Andrew Carter

BENEDICITE

for
S.A.T.B. chorus, children's choir,
and small orchestra

VOCAL SCORE

MUSIC DEPARTMENT

OXFORD
UNIVERSITY PRESS

OXFORD
UNIVERSITY PRESS

Great Clarendon Street, Oxford OX2 6DP, England
198 Madison Avenue, New York, NY10016, USA

Oxford University Press is a department of the University of Oxford.
It furthers the University's aim of excellence in research, scholarship,
and education by publishing worldwide

Oxford is a registered trade mark of Oxford University Press
in the UK and in certain other countries

CONTENTS

NOTE

Benedicite was inspired by the new Benedicite carvings in the restored south transept vault of York Minster. The text comprises a selection of verses from the Benedicite canticle in the *Book of Common Prayer*, freely arranged and added to. In particular, I am indebted to Carol Woollcombe whose initial ideas I have developed in the three sections for children's choir.

Andrew Carter

Benedicite was commissioned by the British Federation of Young Choirs for the 1989 Edinburgh Singing Day. It was first performed on 5 November 1989 in the Queen's Hall, Edinburgh, conducted by Philip Ledger.

The cover photograph is reproduced by kind permission of the
Dean and Chapter of York.
Photographer: Jim Kershaw

The three movements for children's choir may be performed separately as *Bless the Lord*, which is available from the publisher as a separate leaflet. This may also be used as a children's chorus part for performances of the complete work.

INSTRUMENTATION

2 bassoons	timpani
4 horns in F	percussion:
2 trumpets in B flat	cymbals
harp	tam-tam
organ	glockenspiel
strings	waterphone (optional)

Orchestral material is available for hire from the publishers.

Duration: *c.* 35 minutes

to Andrew Fairbairn

Benedicite

1. O all ye works of the Lord
(S.A.T.B.)

Molto ritmico (♩ = 108)

ANDREW CARTER

Printed in Great Britain

OXFORD UNIVERSITY PRESS, MUSIC DEPARTMENT, GREAT CLARENDON STREET, OXFORD OX2 6DP

Lord, praise _____ him and mag - ni - fy him for

e - ver. O ___ ye an - gels ___ of the

Lord, _____ bless ye the Lord,

praise _____ him and mag - ni - fy him for e - ver.

A

S. O ye heav'ns, bless ye the

T. O ye heav'ns, bless ye the

8

2. Green Things
(S.A.T.B.)

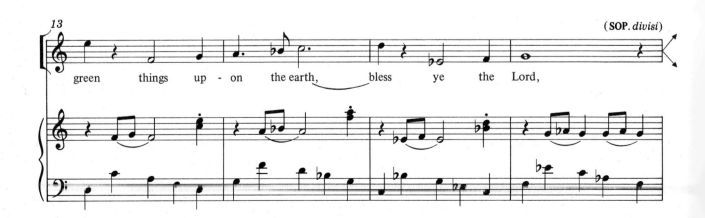

12

13

3. Sun and Moon
(S.A.T.B.)

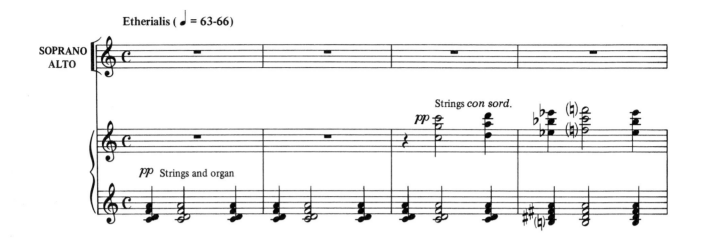

18

4. Badgers and Hedgehogs
(Three-part Children's Choir)

badgers and hedge - hogs, bless the Lord,

O ye dro - me - da - ries and ye dra - gon - flies and did - dy lit - tle dad - dy -

- long - legs, bud - ge - ri - gars and bum - ble - bees and ban - di - coots and

bull - frogs and bad - gers and hedge - hogs, bless the Lord,

1 O ye pa - ra - keets and pe - li - cans and por - cu - pines and

2 O ye wea - sels and wart - hogs and wal - la - bies and

3 O ye dro - me - da - ries and ye dra - gon - flies and did - dy lit - le dad - dy -

5. Ice and Snow
(S.A.T.B.)

28

6. Whales and Waters
(S.A.T.B.)

* There are soli string *glissandi* throughout this 'whale' section.

7. Butterflies and Moths
(Children's Choir in Unison)

creatures, come magnify, magnify the Lord.

All you butterflies, butterflies and moths,

all you hovering and quivering and wondrous

creatures, come magnify, magnify the Lord.

king - fish -ers flash - ing in the morn - ing sun,   come

mag - ni - fy, mag - ni - fy, mag-ni -fy the Lord,   mag- ni - fy, mag-ni - fy, mag - ni -fy the

Lord.

8. Thunder and Lightning
(S.A.T.B.)

52

9. Spirits and Souls
(S.A.T.B.)

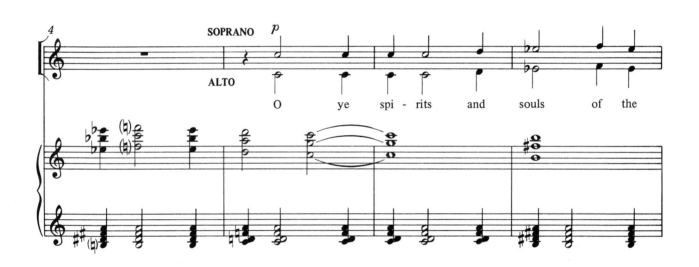

O ye spi - rits and souls of the

right - eous,

56

bless ye the Lord,

O ye child - ren of men.

Attacca 'Grannies and Grandads'

10. Grannies and Grandads
(Children's Choir in Unison)

11. O let the earth bless the Lord

(S.A.T.B. and Children's Choir ad lib.)

62

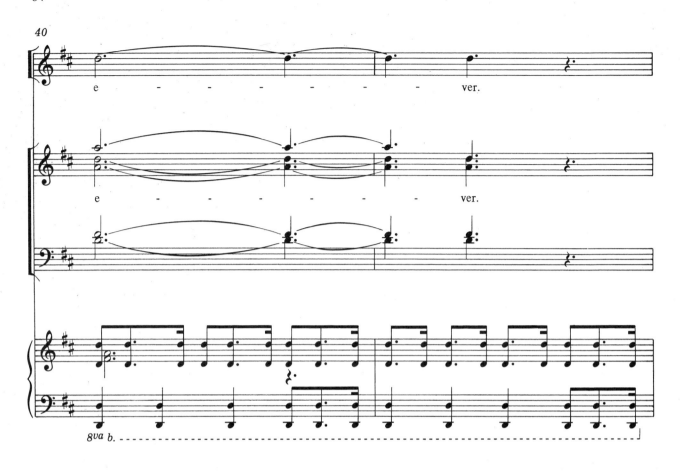

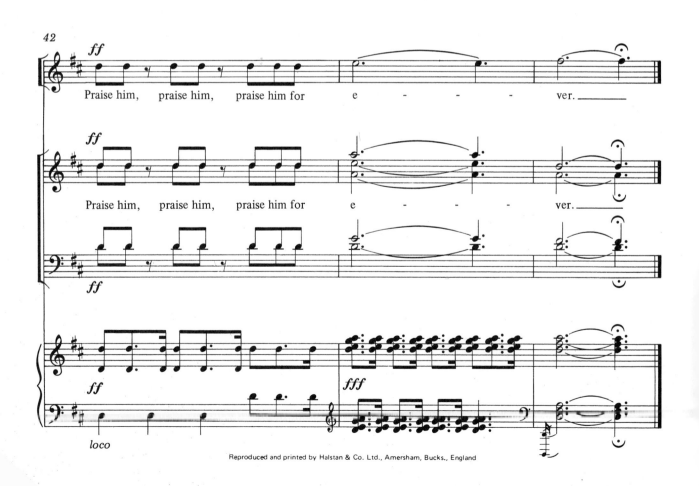